HAMLET IN AUTUMN

Lines Review Editions—2

HAMLET
IN AUTUMN

IAIN CRICHTON SMITH

M. MACDONALD
EDGEFIELD ROAD LOANHEAD MIDLOTHIAN
1972

© Iain Crichton Smith 1972

Published by
M. Macdonald
Edgefield Road, Loanhead, Midlothian

Printed by
Macdonald Printers (Edinburgh) Limited
Edgefield Road, Loanhead, Midlothian

CONTENTS

ON A SUMMER'S DAY

Thus it is.
There is much loneliness
and the cigarette coupons will not save us.

I have studied your face across the draughtsboard.
It is freckled and young.
Death and summer have such fine breasts.

Tanned, they return from the sea.
The colour of sand, their blouses the colour of waves,
they walk in the large screen of my window.

Bacon, whose Pope screams in the regalia
of chairs and glass, dwarf of all the ages,
an hour-glass of ancient Latin,

you have fixed us where we are, cacti able to talk,
twitched by unintelligible tornadoes,
snakes of collapsing sand.

They trail home from the seaside in their loose blouses.
The idiot bounces his ball as they pass.
He tests his senile smile.

THE MOON

The bronze curtains hang at the window.
Between them the moon is shining like a bell.
It is an eye that has been there forever,
a Greek eye older than Pericles.
It looked upon Oedipus and taught him how
the intellect should investigate the flesh,
the rustlings in the shrubbery. It burned
the armour from Greek boxers, those pale statues
that inhabit dense groves. It is the eye
of Sir Apollo, the clear operator,
doctor and sun-god, of the theatre
the radiant master, scooping out the eyes.

OEDIPUS AND OTHERS

The god Apollo scratched out both his eyes.
Tragedy is light too bright to bear.
There were no choices in that azure heaven,
no mercy, only justice. Daughters, sons,
projected death unto the third generation.
Death was everywhere, it was a plague.
The reasonable man became obsessive,
the formal beard was stained with blood, and Creon
forced the young student to the barricades.
From king to rebel, the crystal wheel rotates.
Thin in the light, in vibrant quivering black
Antigone throws the book at Creon, dies
in an ecstasy of longing. Creon says:
"The king must rule, that's what a king is for."
Oedipus sleeps in the groves of wise Athens.
The light burns fiercely on a public stage.
They're all proud germs the theatre must kill.

GOOD AND EVIL

"Good" is not like "yellow" or like "green."
There are no traffic lights that one can stop at.
The soul has many roads and all different.
Frankenstein nails the bride to the wall
and vampires swoop like Zetros. But "good" is not
—nor evil either—clearly what we see
"Good" sits like a nun but is not a nun
it's not the collar of the perishable.
Electricity is waiting in the house.
I enter it from the snowstorm. I switch on
the bulb that glows above my battlefield.
The furniture springs quite clear as we spring clear
from the dreadful dark of strata, murderous pools.
God switched it on and suddenly we shook
in bald vibrations in that merciless light.

OVER AND OVER

They came for him at night in the light of Homer.
Their pistols glittered on the hexameters.

They shot him when the verse was in his mind
of Hector dying, and the chariot wheels

went click click click. In the black leather
he saw Troy burning, and a clear small face

with large round spectacles, barrelled in the light
of the study's genial fireplace. He got up

to pick the book, leathered in black, and then
there was the knock and they came in again.

DEAD FOR A RAT

What snarls
in the corner?
It wants to live
It bares its teeth at you.

It wants to live
more than you do
Its whole body
trembles
with its want to live.

The fur arches from its body
Its green eyes spark
Its lips are drawn back from the teeth
It hates you.

It hates you
more than you hate it.
Hamlet
lie down
in the sound of the trumpet

It quests you Hamlet
Will you go
behind the arras
behind the tapestry
will you go
Hamlet
with all the weight
of your bright thought
upon you?

Will you go Hamlet
in your shuttling armour
in your whirr
of literature
with your French rapier
sparkling, veering?

CAROL AND *HAMLET*
Excerpts from a Sonnet Sequence

Small and small-breasted you scribble in your jotter.
Shakespeare must be known. One needs a Higher
to get a job suited to father's daughter—
or even unsuited. There is a fire
pours through the long windows, causing water
to dance on the wall. From my tall chair
I wonder who perhaps Ophelia was
in her own world apart from Shakespeare's gaze

and the whole lot of them in their private places
before a public tragedy made them pure
and dragged Ophelia from her own oasis
into our own world and into literature
and what you are—beyond hypocrisies—
and I on this unsteady hovering chair.

*   *   *

The light of order (false and yet not false)
Language (not grammar) tells you what I mean
If we could write directly from the pulse . . .
And yet remember how, Venetian
law-court over, Portia to her house
came with her friends: that lovely conversation
in a moonlight more than moonlight, in a peace
more than the peace that one can learn by reason

And Shylock greyly studying his Bible
Had he misread the instructions after all?
We see him sit, intent and miserable.
And then the music starts, the festival
of the successful lovers. Moonlight knows
its own sweet birds, the rest must stick to prose.

*   *   *

13

That leaf you see touching the window now—
I mean in summer—where has it come from?
How old's the tree from which it swam and swam
upward to here? O deep and deep below
this grey stone building can you hear the worm
turning and writhing, hissing, a red fire,
an orchestra of worms about the bare
and brittle skull which still has kept its form?

We ride above them in our little ship.
How many gowns have rustled past that door
containing now an actor, now a bore,
now a great Roman, now a huddled shape,
and yet that leaf is fresher than we are,
green with the green of a transparent grape.

*   *   *

That's why Hamlet always talks of death.
Beyond the ruffs and doublets he saw it clear.
Outgrowing the Renaissance's bright air
he saw instead of wigs the curling wreath.
Below the foam he saw the depths beneath
as you perhaps, a rural visitor,
camping with Girl Guides may see pools where
eels move and flash and coldly whip and writhe

below the dappling sunlight where we live.
I saw it once, an eel, dead-white, upright,
like a blind dancer drifting in the light.
It was so different I couldn't grieve
for such a death so distant and so white
I shivered in the whiteness of my grave.

*   *   *

I too was terrified of words once.
I was so frightened of where words would lead me
that I would walk at night over the stones
(yellow with moonlight) and feel fear beside me
as palpable as a yellow snarling dog
or a yellow rat. The night was wholly yellow.
Inside me a perpetual monologue.
Outside me the whole yellow town was hollow

including the Square, the Post Office (now shut)
the yellow kiosk and each yellow footfall.
I feared each clicking motion of my foot
and felt below me a huge echoing well
where language sent each yellow writhing root
which, had I known it, would grow green and cool.

*   *   *

I've seen you often standing at the wall
when the bride and bridegroom (white and black) come out
and stand at the church door in a kind of doubt
as if they wondered if they'd changed at all
blinking and arranging a bright smile
for the active camera man on his bended knee
aiming at the rose in buttonhole,
the simple dress white as eternity.

And the women with their squawking children stare.
It's as if their heavy lives have origin
in this clear space of wind and sparkling air.
Surely perhaps it's possible to begin
all over again (in a place that's full of sin)
in a moving innocence anyone can share.

*   *   *

As now I see you individual
in a light which is as beautiful and common
as any light which moved about a school
(which after all is an order just as human
as any other we can see or spell)
You are yourself, immaculately Carol,
held in this light of summer's truthful sun.
You hold in your right hand a greenish pen

about to write now in a perfect moment
part of this place and yet yourself as well
transient perhaps but also permanent.
In this clear light you sing like a true bell
and truly yourself are more than ornament
between the visible and the invisible.

DEAR HAMLET

Dear Hamlet, you were pushed beyond your strength
you had a white face and black clothes,
you stood at corners listening.

Surrounded by the voices and wondering what you should do.
The old father whom you admired so much
but who had driven you to Wittenberg
lay murdered.

To avenge him when you did not even like him
(though you admired him) wasn't easy.
He had won so many battles but you,
you had won none.

Poor schoolboy, longing to be like your father,
learning to fence when he had used an axe,
learning philosophy because he hadn't done so.
Words are not enough.

Rushing about from one commandment to another
you were finally focussed as a target
by Claudius, the small and simple man,
yes, he was simple.

So little sufficed him, just a queen, a kingdom,
salutes from guards, dinners with dinner-jackets,
bow-ties and crowns, the glitter of cut-glass,
the colour of poison.

But you, you needed more. That more was death.
You chewed it, fed on it, watched for it in mirrors,
hunted the castle for it, loved it the best
of anything you had known.

How silly Fortinbras was, not to see it
standing behind him just as he took the crown.
That was the moment he began to die
and you began to live.

HOW OFTEN I FEEL LIKE YOU

Ah, you Russians, how often I feel like you
full of ennui, hearing the cry of wolves
on frontiers of green glass.
In the evening
one dreams of white birches and of bears
There are picnics in bright glades and someone talking
endlessly of verse as if mowing grass,
endlessly of philosophy round and round
like a red fair with figures of red soldiers
spinning forever at their "Present Arms."
How long it takes for a letter to arrive.
Postmen slog heavily over the steppes
and drop their dynamite through the letter-box
For something is happening everywhere but here.
Here there are Hamlets and old generals.
Everyone sighs and says "Ekh" and in the stream
a girl is swimming naked among gnats.
This space is far too much for us like time.
Even the clocks have asthma. There is honey,
herring and jam and an old samovar.
Help us, let something happen, even death.
God has forgotten us. We are like fishers
with leather leggings dreaming in a stream.

RUSSIAN POEM

(I)

I am too old for you.
Nevertheless
in summer under a crown of leaves . . .
I am in debt,
a kind of Hamlet.
Nevertheless,
Sonia, you are beautiful.
I've left my Jewish wife
mooning from piano to vodka.
She coughs all night.
You do not know the guilt . . .
Here in the sunshine it is fine,
you in your white dress. . . .
People, such people.
Generals
with false red faces
booming like snipes.
Old uncles, aunts,
surplus to requirements
Sonia,
there was a time
when I had ideals
Now my back is broken.
I feel nothing, Sonia,
even should you put
lightly your hand in mine,
even should you kiss
I'd not awaken.
Sonia, I'm afraid
of this old skin.

(II)

Ennui covers the land.
Broken fences.
Russia is full of broken fences.
Pigs root in the muck.
Grandfathers roast themselves on stoves.
Ash on their waistcoats.

Something is bound to happen.
They click their heels like toys,
kiss over olives
fine, and cared-for, hands.
There's something I'm hearing.

Great cannon in small ears.
The stone heads tremble.
The wolves trouble our wit.
They are seething like water.

(III)

Hear us, Philosophy will not save us.
In our salons we have talked the 'soul' to death.

Our cigar smoke snakes from the orchard
where the apples ripen and the small hands

shine.

Our glasses reflect the sunset. Our monocles
have a raw glare. The uncles

twinkle like robins.

We have talked the 'soul' to death. Now as the sun goes down
we shiver and go in.

(IV)

Gogol, how your troika sparkled down our leaf-fringed lanes.
You stopped at the most absurd houses
where everyone was himself and dullness sparkled like genius.

Moral bachelor, what has happened to you? You have run to history
for protection. You have abandoned your people.
You have run your little troika into the wilderness.

(V)

In the siding the red light veins his beard.
The rails run elsewhere, hard and narrowing.
Our land breathed through you. Now you are breathless.
Your soul is blown sideways by the steam.

I look down the track at the raw torches
wandering hither and thither. What do I see?
Is it the mad city face of Dostoevsky?

(VI)

'We shall soon go to Moscow,' say the sisters
watching the great bear at the edge of the forest
bumbling along, so neat and strong.

There is the taste of autumn in the air,
the taste of aisles and pillars and of lemon,
the taste of tall clear glasses on the lawn.

The bear trots amiably among the steeples
They watch him through their telescopes so mild,
so cuddly and ingenuous. He stares

back through the telescope. And the trees shake.
The glasses shake, the ringless pale hands,
and Moscow in their silk sways without sound.

(VII)

Sometimes I think of the Cossacks wolfing their hunks of flesh
and the Poles equably turning
with soundless screams over their evening fires.

They would piss into the open mouths of the dead
but they polished their ikons.

How terrified we would be if in our salons
a sabre should be reflected
and a happy face smiling above the moustache,
a murderous childlike face.

I imagine our glass walls cracking before them,
our women being raped among smelling salts,
and two heels drumming on the fine silk.

Ah, our Hamlet, where are you? How your soul trembles
like a tiny drop of dew on a gibbet

as these riders scratch their raw necks,
as they spit bountifully on to the marble,
as they unhitch their belts and belch comfortably
munching legs of chicken, gazing at the wrenched limbs.

(VIII)

The idiot stands on the pavement
with a rainbow-coloured ball in his hands,
a large ball which he kneads continually.
He has a large Teutonic head,
his hair is crew-cut
and he has big thick lips.
Hour after hour he stands
legs spread apart
in a dull masterful strut.
He's squat, short, a boy,
but his hair is grey in the light
He is old, this idiot
far older than his toy.

(IX)

I hear that he came in a sealed train.
Yesterday I heard him
His head is like the round stone balls you see on gateposts.

When his arm jabs the air, you hear cannon.
The whirling snow settles on the ground.

His head is a bell tolling for theses,
articles, students, appendices and "questions."

He has simplified the world like an assassin.
Where his barrel points is where evil is.

(X)

Sonia, my fine ghost,
I see you among the rifles.
You were saying "What need of a psychiatrist?
He would only stare at my wrist."

Sonia, you were a sign of the times
a young girl vibrating out of phase.
I see you wearing white slacks,
legs spread apart,
reading old leaves.

Sonia, you were a generator
bouncing on a piece of waste ground.

Sonia, it has come at last.
The newspapers have gone mad.
They are punching out Reality.

If I do not die now I shall die.

Sonia, I stretch out my hand to you.
I am afraid but I stretch out my hand to you.
Sonia, let us follow the wind.

LYING ILL

Lying here for three days I might ask,
Why should I rise?

The unknowing germs have manoeuvred their way through me.
One wouldn't say they are clever: merely a weather
under which I drizzle.

I have let my hot head lie on its pillow.
Passive threads have hauled towards my window
these hills, that tree, that sky.

That tree. I have noticed how it shivers totally.
It palpitates like a sponge, like the brain
composed of its trillion cells.

Someone rings the small doorbell. I don't care.
Through this dough a hole is drilled, this mound
turns over on its side.

Why should I rise?
thought the dinosaur feeling the sharp white torch
of man's cold mind drilling

through the vast dough, scales, assembling ages,
that warmed its little squeak within that mountain
ash-coloured and distraught.

And the jungle felt it, that white piercing mind
crippling trees, punching the raw snouts back,
a torch among chimneys in the night-time
a being that cannot sleep,

but is condemned to rise.

HOTEL DINING ROOM

Our mouths work in the hotel dining room,
like mice nibbling, like mice nibbling forever
at the fat cheese on the edge of the wooden trap,
The chilled wine cools us like academies
clustered with the black grapes of professors,
but we know the forest, we have known the forest,
we have climbed the trees nibbling and looking down.
The waitress wears a handkerchief of flame,
the propped menu speaks of literature,
the poetry of the parkland and the streams,
But the voice behind you has known foxes
the rank stink of them, the sound of Brahms.
We nibble at the cheese, stunningly caught
in all this glass, these coiffures wired with light.

FILMS

These serious tedious Scandinavian films

forests like chessboards where the heroine
chased by a rapist jumps from square to square:

games played with souls among the birchen chairs
contemporary spindly: and at night

handfuls of blood left on the white pillow.

Strange how on entering the street again
one is appeased by such inferior drama
steam of the ice cold air. The looming buses
are warm red boxes, and the promenaders

parade in green, their skulls as white as snow.

PARTY

Cigarette ends mounting slowly in the ashtray,
so many Hamlets speaking all at once.
'Polonius is a fool to have such power.'
I leaf through Bacon's paintings in the corner,
a butcher's shop of graduated screams.

Now they are dancing on the charred carpet.
You can tell the lost ones from their stiff arms.

The others sway to the music just like snakes.
"He's nice to me but never says he loves me.
He strokes his car's flanks over and over."
She waggles her bum, a green suburban mermaid,
flicking her fingers, Venus of the record player
half hidden by the fog, the swirling grey.

DIPPING YOUR SPOON . . .

Dipping your spoon in the mash of TV
palls. Everything palls. Spy and detective stories,

watching your cold small face on its seventh gin,
hearing the ringing jokes from bell-like faces,

writing great novels on white tablecloths.
What is given is not enough to make us swing
happily on branches or to climb
these long stone stairs, watches bobbing on chains.
We want the Commandments from the gritty deserts

and shadowy ghosts in their post-Renaissance frames,
our underwater programmes. We want your Commandments
suited to a pastoral land in green,
the extinct shepherds with their pilgrim staffs,
their clouds of white sheep and visiting angels
perching on branches with their fathomless eyes.

SHANE

He comes out of some place where he has invented justice.
What is good has to be protected by guns
and that is why he's so sombre. Why his silence
grows on the bustling housewife who asks about fashions.
He has learned a style from evil, he has honed it on
conflict. He knows that books will not save
the innocent man. He stands by the fence
undazzled yet alert, expecting evil
as natural as sunlight. Yet with what grief he goes
to find his guns again, to relearn his quickness.

CHAPLIN

Everything seems pasted on,
the baggy trousers, the moustache,
The teeth shine over a smashed dish.
The silence helps him. Watch his pose,
the V-shaped broken boots. The doors
swing shut to hide him. He fights
the moving elevators,
cycling upstream.
His cane is thin as a stem.
One could not lean on it. He pulls
thick cultures down. He trudges on
to a thriving emptiness.

END OF SCHOOLDAYS

Captains, this is your last day in school.
You won't wear these helmets any more.
Do you not hear the whisper in the triumph,
like a suspect heart? Do you not see
how Mr Scott, though kind, is harried
by voices inaudibly calling from his house.

Look out on the fields. Never again will you see
such a sweet greenness, as of colours leaving
a place where they've been happy for a while.
The harness is turning now to other horses.
Laughter comes up the road and mounts the brae.
The names on the doors are rewriting themselves.

Never mind, the music will not leave you
or not completely. Sometimes in a betrayal,
in the middle of a deal just turning rancid,
after the fifth gin, the fifth fat hand,
the cloudy globes, set on the cloth, you'll hear it,

the music of your Ideal, quietly humming
in locker-rooms that smell of sweat and rain.
You'll be coming home in a warm and eerie light,
legs tall and willowy, in your hand the cup,
shaking a little, in your flabby hand
the trembling cup, in your old grasping hand.

NAPOLEON

So you came back and then stretched wide your arms
to Ney, the best and bravest. Your Last Stand.
A Hollywood producer minus cigar,
a plumper frog than when you went away.
The stage was set with twenty thousand cannon.
You swung in your chair with your scenario
shouting Action Action. It was Waterloo.
You drove your upright columns to the charge
chewed by the piercing of your early star
that wished to be away. They never come back.
Athletes, boxers, actors, they never come back,
they never gain their vibrant souls again,
the fat will cover them. Seasick you lay
stretched in your deckchair at St Helena
smoked glasses misted by the endless spray,
the starlets flown forever like the swallows
to other nests and salons. Your great head
gloomed like a sagging cannon. In your brain
the tall beaked bony body wandered forever,
the irrational unbeatable slow power
far too insensitive to know defeat.
It was on him your subtle genius broke,
on the dense ignorance of life itself,
the earth his cannon threw up in the air.

FOR KEATS

Genius is so strange,
you were in so many ways ordinary
in so many ways wounded like us.

But the vase beckons—
continually the vase beckons—
the imperfect bird sings
in the brown mortal leaves.

Poor Tom dies in the white linen.
Sore throats! Do nightingales have sore throats?
In the nightingale's pure notes
What eloquent disease?

Happily to seek the classic—
that land without fatigue—
that which stands like the rocks of Staffa
black remarkable architecture of the sea
solider than weeping Skye.

Than the grass of summer,
devotees of England's spas,
the irritabilities of the second rate,
the helmet bruised and vain.

Fighting the scree, to arrive at Autumn,
innocent impersonal accepted
where the trees do not weep like gods
but are at last themselves.

Bristly autumn, posthumous and still,
the crowning fine frost on the hill
the perfect picture blue and open-eyed
with the lakes as fixed as your brother's eyes,
autumn that will return

and will return and will return, however
the different delicate vase revolves
in the brown mortal foliage, in the woods
of egos white as flowers.

THIS IS THE TIME OF THE BODY . . .

This is the time of the body not the mind
You sway in time. Your eyes are closed and glowing.
The scholarly helmets in the armchairs turn
to Dionysus in his wheel of hair
and Greece thuds hollowly to the ordered legions

crewcut and lotioned. Let the dance begin
which brings hypnosis to the stoa and
the loose and amateur stars into the hall.
The philosophers are halfway here and there
half satyrs and half Saturns in their minds

Let the dance begin, the music of the spheres
distorted by the stormy Goths is heard
only in private rooms whose walls are shaken.
O in a trance of dancing see them share
their bodies with the spaces of the light

though still Narcissi in their secret moons
lilies and schoolgirls, virgins of their joy
hysteric against matronhood. They move
as riotous stalks might move and writhe and sway,
mindless of mind whose needles pierce and sew.

FOR JOHN MACLEAN, HEADMASTER, AND CLASSICAL AND GAELIC SCHOLAR

(I)

The coloured roses fade along the wall.
How shall we live? How perfectly they fall,
the October leaves in yellow, how exact
the woods appear, so married to the fact
of their own unwilled and accurate funeral
without interrogation. In this tract

the dazzling hearse has led us to, we stand,
hats in our hands. The serious piper plays
"The Lament for the Children" and we hear the bound
and ribboned bouquets thudding. Then we take our ways
to the waiting cars across unechoing ground

or over crackling gravel. It remains,
the body in the casket, and begins
its simple mineral weathering. We return
to our complex human burning. What we mourn
changes as we mourn it, and routines
wed and enring us as we move and burn.

(II)

For you it was the case that Homer lived
in our fluorescence, that Ulysses homed
through our stained and plaguey light, that Hector grieved
in his puncturable armour, that engraved
even in Skye was marble which consumed
the bodies of live Greeks who shaped and carved

contemporary sculpture. Under leaves
which dappled your warm garden (as the groves
of autumnal classic Greece) you turned a page
or made an emendation in a passage.
Exactitude's a virtue, so believes
the inveterate scholar. Happy who can judge

35

evil as a hiatus or a false
quantity in harmony, who knows
that what protects us from the animals
is language healthy as a healthy pulse
and that our moral being can like prose
be manifestly tested where it fails.

(III)

I know that it is waning, that clear light
that shone on all our books and made them white
with unanswerable grammar. That the slaves
sustained our libraries and that the wolves
and watchful eagles nourished an elite
and that the elegant and forceful proofs

of their geometers will not suffice.
I know that Athene is wandering now,
dishevelled in the shrubbery, and the nurse
beckons at evening to her. Gods rehearse
their ruined postures and the ruined brow
reflects from mirrors not of fire but ice

and that our brute Achilles drives his wheels
across the gesturing shadows: and that kneels
to cheering legions Aphrodite: packs
are watching Ajax hacking with his axe
inanely the pale sheep: and shady deals
illuminate Odysseus's tracks.

(IV)

You were a teacher also: what we've learned
is also what we teach: and what we are
cannot be hidden, though we walk black-gowned
along the radiant corridors, profound
in serious scholarship and that precious star
proposed by art or conscience. Where you burned

exactitude prevailed, the rule of Rome,
the gravitas of Brutus and his calm,
his stoic tenderness, his love of books,
his principles and practice. For the Dux
stands in his place, the overwhelming psalm
enchants him wholly among clean-limbed Greeks,

and if you touch him he gives out true coin.
Echo on echo, pupils make a world
which is their bronze and yours, and they will join
link on bright link to make the legions shine
with ethics and with elegance. The absurd
becomes a simple weather, clear and fine.

(V)

The October leaves are falling. None condemns
their seasonal abdication. What consumes
their crowns and robes is natural, a law
that's common to the weasel and the crow.
They hear no music of the funeral drums
and no corteges shade the way they go

no mountains brood, nor does the sharp wind mourn
nor tragic clouds move slowly. For the ice
steadily thickens over lake and corn.
In this pure azure there's no paradise
nor the hell nor purgatory that we devise
lest in the world we shiver and we burn

without the falcon's unhistorical aim,
its brutal beak, the momentary tomb
of its spontaneous moments. Or the sheep
that grazes in its own forgetful sleep
or the barbarians that struck at Rome,
its pompous destiny and shadowed hope.

(VI)

Though it is finished now, that scholarship,
though vases crack and hourly we may graze
on superficial quanta: though we sleep
abandoned to disorder, and the days
are flashes of small light: and what we praise
is transient and odd, we yet may keep

pictures of autumn, graver, more restrained,
with a finer balance of the weighty mind,
a wind from Rome and Greece which held our course
steady to a harbour where salt oars
received their justice and to scales assigned
the soul would shiver with a stronger force

which now in neon vibrates. But in light
(let it be legend) accompanied the leaves
to their natural assignations and the fruit
bowed to a holy earth. The swan that moves
in reedy waters bows its neck. The waves
receive it, flesh and shadow, day and night.

(VII)

So with your battered helmet let you be
immersed in golden autumn as each tree
accepts its destiny and will put by
its outworn crown, its varying finery,
and let the humming of the latest bee
bear its last honey home. Beneath this sky

the hexagonal coffin crowned with flowers restores
your body to the earth from which we came
to build our shaking ladders. What was yours
was no phantasmal order, and your name
planted in this place held to its aim
from wider deeper origins. If there were pyres

then a pyre you should have had, and lictors too.
And phantom legions. In this perfect blue
imagine therefore flame that's amber, yellow,
leaves of good flame, volumes that burn and glow,
the foliage of your autumn, where you grew
and where you are buried in the earth you know.

YOU ARE AT THE BOTTOM OF MY MIND

Without my knowing it, you are at the bottom of my mind, like one who visits the bottom of the sea with his helmet and his two great eyes: and I do not know properly your expression or your manner after five years of the showers of time pouring between you and me.

Nameless mountains of water pouring between me, hauling you on board, and your expression and manners in my weak hands. You went astray among the mysterious foliage of the sea-bottom in the green half-light without love.

And you will never rise to the surface of the sea, even though my hands should be ceaselessly hauling, and I do not know your way at all, you in the half-light of your sleep, haunting the bottom of the sea without ceasing and I hauling and hauling on the surface of the ocean.

GOING HOME

Tomorrow I will go home to my island, trying to put a world into forgetfulness. I will lift a fistful of earth in my hands or I will sit on a hillock of the mind watching "the shepherd with his sheep."

There will ascend (I presume) a thrush. A dawn or two will rise. A boat will be lying in the glitter of the western sun and water will be running through the world of the similes of my intelligence. But I will be thinking (in spite of that) of the great fire that is behind our thoughts, Nagasaki and Hiroshima, and I will hear in a room by myself the ghost of every guilt, the ghost of each time I walked past the wounded man on the stony road, the ghost of nothingness scrutinising my dumb room with distant face, till the island is an ark rising and falling on a great sea and no one knowing whether the dove will ever return, and people talking and talking to each other, and the rainbow of forgiveness in their tears.

THE STONES OF CALLANISH

At the stones of Callanish yesterday I heard one woman saying to another: "This is where they burnt the children in olden times." I did not see druids among the planets nor sun nor robe: but I saw a beautiful blue wall like heaven cracking and children with skin hanging to them like the flag in which Nagasaki was sacrificed.

THE FOOL

In the dress of the fool, the two colours that have tormented me —English and Gaelic, black and red, the court of injustice, the reason for my anger, and that fine rain from the mountains and those grievous storms from my mind streaming the two colours together so that I will go with poor sight in the one colour that is so odd that the King himself will not understand my conversation.

ON A BEAUTIFUL DAY

From the stones the wildcat is watching the world. The hare shakes like a lily. The hawk and the lark are in the same mirror and the sun shining and the grass growing. The wildcat is drinking champagne over his teeth. The hare is halted, listening with ears like doors. The hawk is sitting on its wings drinking the wind and the lark singing like a record in a Gaelic cloud.

GAELIC SONGS

I listen to these songs
from a city studio.
They belong to a different country,
to a barer sky,
to a district of heather and stone.
They belong to the sailors
who kept their course
through nostalgia and moonlight.
They belong to the maidens
who carried the milk in pails
home in the twilight.
They belong to the barking of dogs,
to the midnight of stars,
to the sea's terrible force,
exile past the equator.
They belong to the sparse grass,
to the wrinkled faces,
to the houses sunk in the valleys,
to the mirrors
brought home from the fishing.

Now they are made of crystal
taking just a moment
between two programmes
elbowing them fiercely
between two darknesses.

IN THE COUNTRY

Everyone is so nice.
In the shops they smile as in a spoon.
On the stage
they unconvincingly imitate sin.

Their drugged footballers wade through grasses.
As if in an aquarium
the striped unbrilliant fish
rise and sing in their parish.

The old ladies are preserved
on mantlepieces of the mind.
The lawyers in their braces bend
among the red and white.

A sleep has fallen on the world.
A sleep of niceness has fallen
out of heaven
on the limbs of the living.

The tall policeman strolls
down street on shiny street,
his truncheon hidden in light,
a tamed spider.

Today there is no wind
After the lightning bolts the flesh
the exhausted bodies lie
face upwards on the sand

hearing the thunder of the jet
a vicious hornet
which leaves a long trail of white
in the space it has just left.

NOT TO ISLANDS

Not to islands ever returning now
with much of hope or comfort. Not to you,
asleep in the blue sky of TV,
Lewis or Uist, Harris or Tiree.
Shadows assemble from America
where once the moors were silent, where once
the sea's monotony was experience.
Where once we drowsed on the hot flowers in summer
staring across the ocean to where lay
America invisible, unknown,
in ignorant mirrors hanging upside-down
invincibly at peace, the bell-like day.

FOR ANN IN AMERICA IN THE AUTUMN

When the wind dies in New Jersey
and it is the Fall
and the horses canter home to their stables
over the late grass, the late leaves,
remember how it is here in this small
place without air far from New England's Lowell.

Gently the leaves spiral as they fall.
The logfire sparkles red as a new apple.
O hills of the Far Country you're so blue
and dead and quiet. The old clouds drift through
the old mind. The weighted earth prevails.
We're hauled towards gravity by the worn heels.

Something regrets us. Something we regret.
I smell your woodsmoke, it is pure and tart.
Here by this shore the sea turns round again.
My head swings dully in its leaves of pain.
What horses leave me in this frosty Fall—
the girls ride westwards on their rising wheel.

THE RETURN

Continuous music in the restaurant
The Chinese girl reading a Chinese book,
a Chinaman with hands behind his back.
Now that he listened closely it was Gaelic
but with a slant and eastern tone to it.
Inside the ruby of the reddish light
he heard the minister's perpetual chant.

He signalled for the girl who quietly spoke
the language that he knew as if she meant
to be as always, kindly and polite.

There was a man his hands behind his back
before the fire. His name began with Mac . . .
He couldn't remember for the soothing music.
The girl was sitting at the table, slack
pen in her slack hand, thinking of work.
A test tomorrow, homework for tonight. . . .
He saw it was Mary. In the reddish light
she looked much paler greener in the slip
she wore for the gymnasium. It was dark
in the corner where she was, just by the phone.
It hadn't rung but he could hear one speak.
The music varied from its monotone.
It was the First World War song, "The White Swan."
The man went over and leaned towards her.
Then very slowly he removed her pen
her book her slip her face. And she was gone.

A girl swam towards him. She held out a tray
a piece of paper on it. She was yellow.
She didn't smile, a robot of the light.
The Chinaman was standing, looking straight
in front of him at the window opposite.
The room was silent empty glowing red . . .
The girl went through a door which swung and swung

Around him hummed the queer continuous song.

IN THE CHINESE RESTAURANT

Because we'd never go there, it was good,
those years together. We'd never need to go
though we could talk of it and so we were
happy together in a place we'd made
so small and airless that we couldn't leave.
But we could think of it and say, 'Perhaps
we'll go there someday.' But we could not go
for as we lived so we'd lost all the maps.
It grew more perfect as the slow years passed
as if we were there already. One fine day
we'd find it all around us if we looked.
We would be in it, even old and grey.

So that, one night, in that late restaurant
with Chinese waiters round us we picked up
the menu in Chinese and understood
every single word of it. It was
a revelation when the waiters smiled.
They looked so clear as the glasses slowly filled.

RETURN

I lived in that room fifteen years ago
high above the roses. I see a maid
moving in white beyond the pale window.
Strangers own it now and a wooden sign
swings to and fro, swings endlessly to and fro,

saying "Bed and Breakfast." "Vacancy." It was
a time I have forgotten. Better forget.
The lights turn elsewhere now. And the tall stairs
creak to the English visitors who bring
their happy Easter faces to the north.

We change. All changes. As I turn away
there's a wedding on, just at the small church there.
New children bend after old pennies.
A door bangs shut. A black car slides away
in snowflakes flung from open gloved hands.

Opposite it, the mill is still standing.
Black pails, brown pipes, new planks and knotted wood.
The sawdust rises, wave on wave, like meal.
My arm aches for a plane, a saw, a hammer,
for anything solid in the sparkling stream.

OUR MESS TINS . . .

Our mess tins soggy with stew
we sat around the campfire
in the October woods.
The unmilitary owls hooted
and the trees
learned the embrace of ice.

Such millions of stars shining
such a brown
ending to autumn,
and our khaki
imitating a season
that would surely die.

Soldiers of the queen.
The trees were abdicating,
laying aside their crowns
and rustling finery
in that court intense
with a smoky burning

Tang of autumn leaves.
How like the legions
late in the late woods
of a decaying Empire
we ringed the pale campfire
with our rusty badges.

Young, so young.
Hard to remember
that bewildered boyhood
holding that cold tin
fork knife and spoon
among the acorns

among the autumn woods
all sentimental
lying on coats later
while down our white throats
the radiant moon poured
its white powder.

THE SMALL SNAGS

The small snags tug at us. The flag will not unfold
glorious in the weather of our triumph.
It is the small snags that won't let go.
For if the flag unfolds and leaves the earth
and is pure spirit, a wide heavenly cloth,
then earth will not remember us but fade
with its arrangement of small serious weasels,
its rats with clear green eyes, its stoats and foxes,
the thickets that entangle as we move.

Let not the flag unfold too widely, let not
the hero in his brilliance, let not
the silk unwind its soul's advertisements,
but be like clothes snarled in the summer hedges
where the birds sing clearly from their dying mouths
and the owl snaps through its folds.

CHILDREN IN WINTER

In the dark mornings
the orange coloured children
test the black streets
hand in hand.

The darkness pours down.
The moon is leaning backwards
like an exhausted woman.

They fade into their future,
like small orange sails
breasting the darkness.

LEAR AND CARROLL

Those child-loving nonsense-writing Victorian uncles,
how they sadden us with their large heads and mild eyes,
with their imaginary bestiaries set in the tall avenues
of the shadows which destroyed them, the long skirts of windless
    days.

THE TAPE RUNS

The tape runs
bearing its weight of poems
conversations
echoes of past rhymes.

Sometimes I think that time
is odder
than any order
for to gain one future
is to lose another

Calmly the tape runs
The fruit of dead voices
composes
itself on the brown wheels.

They return to us
over and over
in this calm weather
of continuous hum

Dear dead voices
dear dignified ones
I see your bones
in this green focus

narrowing widening
the grass of your burying
small set green window
pulsing with a whole life.

GIVE ME YOUR HAND

Give me your hand.
Do you not feel it,
the first chill of autumn?
The azure is razor sharp
the brown nostalgic.

There is no noise.
The light is single
under the uncrowned trees
It is beaten like steel
interrupted by litter

Ah the queens are all gone
with their brocade and silken
garments of the summer.
Without their fripperies
they are naked like us

We are at zero.
There is no babbling
of water over stones.
The stones are bearded
with unshaken moss.

The trees are thermometers
almost transparent
There is no sap
or it's descended
to an absent country.

Give me your hand,
we are two orphans
with large blue eyes
in a story of Andersen's
on an autumnal journey.

BY THE SEA IN AUTUMN

The mussels clamp their miniature helmets to
the salty rocks. The sea comes pouring down.

It is the war they shelter from, my fathers,
it is the war these summers long ago
the blossoms of the hedges and of bone,
the horses and the seagulls in the blue

You in your yellow dress peering about
your shells and fools gold in your sprayed glasses
are a permission of that resonance
that sucks the mussels from their parapets.

The large continuous ghosts come pouring down.
By these sieged heads you bend your luminous dress.

FAIRY STORY

Snow. Much snow. Ice. A cottage.
The small gnomes were digging underground,
their tiny spades shining in the lamplight.
The world of fairy stories. And I turned

another page. The whole alphabet
was lovely icicles, needles. You were there
whitely lying on a white bed.
There was a crown of blossom on your hair

syringes, rings, blue Icelandic nurses.
The small crystal radios were hung
among reindeer, birches, bearish furs.
The cottage crumples slowly, it is going

down to a white plate like blancmange.
The gnomes are digging busily. I see
their neon spades flickering, their hands
are small and yellow. In reality

I turn another page, crackling like ice.
Oh love, how long ago it all was
The white earth is pleading with black heaven
demanding justice, demanding more than justice.

CHRISTMAS, 1971

There's no snow this Christmas . . . there was snow
When we received the small horses and small cart,
brothers together all those years ago.
There were small watches made of liquorice
surrealist as time hung over chairs.
I think perhaps that when we left the door
of the white cottage with its fraudulent icing
we were quite fixed as to our different ways.
Someone is waving with black liquorice hands
at the squashed windows as the soundless bells
and the soundless whips lash our dwarf horses forward.
We diverge at the road-end in the whirling snow
never to meet but singing, pulling gloves
over and over our disappearing hands.

THE LETTER

Here is my letter out of the mirror
God who created us.

Why did you put the rabbit in the belly of the fox?
Why did you put man in the box of his days?
Why did you build us of frail bones?

Why did you give us hearts
to suffer hubbub and sorrow,
why aren't they like watches
small, circular, golden?

Why did you leave the eagle alone
in a nest of clouds
suspended on rays,
hammered with nails?

Why did you not make angels or beasts of us
with cold wings, with barbaric heads?
Why did you praise the sea in front of us
with a wide meaningless face?

In the mirror
a boxer's face,
in the mirror
a rusty helmet.

In the mirror is your book with a steel band,
with an edge sharp as a razor.

In the mirror there is one rose,
our hope growing,
red, shaken by the winds,
in a circle of dew.

IN THE TIME OF THE USELESS PITY

In the time of the useless pity I turned away
from your luminous clock-face in the hopeless dark,
appealing to me greenly, appealing whitely.
Nothing I could do, I had tried everything,
lain flat on the rug, fluttered my spaniel paws,
offered you my house like an unlocked crystal—
and so it came, the time of the useless pity
when the roots had had enough of you, when they slept,
elaborating themselves by themselves
when they shifted over from yours, seeking a place
different from yours to burst through and to pierce
with a royal purple, straight and delicate: sails
of the suave petals unfurling at the mast.

FINIS NOT TRAGEDY

All is just. The mouth you feed turns on you
if not truly fed, the machine clicks
accurately in a new house.

The will that you abolished stands slackly
when you need it most, the vanquished
muscles will not answer.

The machine, powered by history, clicks
shut like a filing cabinet and on it
you read Finis not Tragedy.

Nothing is there that wasn't there.
No memos that you haven't read
over and over again

when your skull-faced secretary stood smiling
as you tore papers into little pieces
and hummed through your clenched teeth

and turning you said to him "Remember honour.
Tell the story as it really was."
But he is silent, smiling.

EVERYTHING IS SILENT

Everything is silent now
before the storm.
The transparent walls tremble.
You can hear the very slightest hum
of a stream miles away.

The silence educates your ear.
The threat is palpable.
You can hear the boots beyond the mountains.
You can hear the breathings of feathers.
You can hear the well of your heart.

You know what it is that permits the walls,
that allows the ceiling,
that lets the skin cling to your body,
that mounts the spiral
of your beholden bones.

That sorrow is a great sorrow
and leaves you radiant
when the tempest has passed
and your vases are still standing
and your bones are stalks in the water.

THIS GOODBYE

This goodbye
was the closing of two doors,
the dimming of two circles.

This goodbye
was not an assembling of
precious souvenirs.

This goodbye
happened so quickly I
was not aware of it.

It was just that I was not looked at.
It was just
an injustice of the glass.